Encounter

20 interactive Bible studies
for small groups

A resource for small group members
and leaders

Empowering People

Other titles in this series:

Empowering People
Help! I am leading part of my Small Group
Small Groups—an Introduction

Encounter

Published and distributed by:

Cell UK Ministries,
Highfield Oval,
Harpenden, Herts.
AL5 4BX

First published in the UK in 2018

ISBN: 978-1-902144-53-5

Contents

	Page
Introduction	4
The Kingdom of God *by Trevor Withers*	6
Fruitfulness *by Laurence Singlehurst*	8
Empowered to love *by Laurence Singlehurst*	10
Empowered discipleship *by Laurence Singlehurst*	12
Cracked pots...letting the light shine out *by Trevor Withers*	14
Self image *by Laurence Singlehurst*	16
Encourage one another *by Trevor Withers*	18
Blessed to be a blessing *by Trevor Withers*	20
Having co-workers *by Trevor Withers*	22
Prayer *by Laurence Singlehurst*	24
Prayer for others *by Laurence Singlehurst*	26
Hearing God in ordinary places *by Trevor Withers*	28
Guidance *by Laurence Singlehurst*	30
Our view of people *by Laurence Singlehurst*	32
Our view of people in the workplace *by Laurence Singlehurst*	34
The Unknown God *by Trevor Withers*	36
People of peace *by Trevor Withers*	38
Make the most of every opportunity *by Trevor Withers*	40
The power of questions *by Trevor Withers*	42
Hospitality *by Laurence Singlehurst*	44
Other resources	46
About the authors	49
Notes	50

Introduction

Our hope in writing these Bible study outlines is that God will stir you to live out the values of his kingdom in every area of your life.

How can we help and support each other as we seek to live within the kingdom of God? This is our theme through these group outlines. We hope that as a result of the way your group works with these twenty meeting suggestions you will see change in individuals and in your group.

We have added our thoughts about each passage and seek to encourage your discussion with questions, but it is in the response time where we hope you will focus a majority of your time together. It is not so much about what we know, but how we are going to respond and change as a result of what we know. This is not so much about a Bible study where you acquire more information, but more about the application of what comes up in response to the text. As James says; *'Do not merely listen to the word, and so deceive yourselves. Do what it says.'* (James 1:22)

Encouraging honesty and openness in the group will be an important part of growth. The atmosphere in the group, the level of trust and commitment to confidentiality will be a foundation for this. The support and love of the group is invaluable as individuals grapple with their issues. Giving opportunity for updates over the weeks will also help.

How you pray for each other and your concerns will depend on what is comfortable for your group. Prayer can mean many things to people and using a variety of styles would be helpful, from symbolism to silence and honest sharing to sustained, ongoing persistence.

On a few occasions specific ideas for prayer have been added in the 'Response' section, but it is up to you how and when you decide as a group to pray for individuals around the issues that come up.

Take your time.

This is not about completing the course or getting to the next thing, it's about creating space and an atmosphere where God can be at work in us and through us. Give yourselves permission to revisit areas that have come up. Use the questions to unpack things and explore the often hidden depths of the kingdom of God.

Three ways you could use this booklet:

1. Work through the sessions as they are in the booklet; we have put them together so they build on each other.

2. Use a few at a time to intersperse your normal pattern and so spread them out over a year or so.

3. Dip into them when you have occasion to. Many small groups follow the Sunday teaching of the church they are part of. Sometimes the Sunday content is not applicable so these encounter outlines can be used.

If you are planning to use them as a series then can we encourage you to take a break part way through and talk about how the sessions have stirred you and the changes in perspective they have brought about.

Laurence Singlehurst and
Trevor Withers

The Kingdom of God

The Mustard Seed, Matthew 13 : 31-33

He (Jesus) presented another parable to them, saying, "The kingdom of heaven is like a mustard seed, which a man took and sowed in his field; and this is smaller than all other seeds, but when it is full grown, it is larger than the garden plants and becomes a tree, so that the birds of the air come and nest in its branches."

Read the passage several times, leaving space in between each reading so that it settles with the group.

Thoughts from this passage

The kingdom of God is a major theme for Jesus. He returns to it again and again, so we thought this series should start with it. This is just one of the many examples that Jesus uses to describe what the kingdom is like. A parable according to the Oxford English dictionary is; 'a simple story used to illustrate a moral or spiritual lesson, as told by Jesus in the Gospels.' So what does this story tell us about the kingdom of God and our part in it?

I just want to pick up on two thoughts here:

The first is simply that the mustard seed, like all seeds, has to cease to be in seed form so that the mustard tree can grow from it. It enables something else to grow and flourish, although having the same DNA.

What grows is larger than other plants in the garden and becomes a tree.

The second is that the 'birds of the air come and nest in its branches'. If you have ever had a bird table in your garden you will know that it is difficult to only allow certain types of birds to feed from it and almost impossible to stop the local squirrel population polishing the lot off before a bird of any kind has even appeared! The reason I mention this is that all kinds of wandering birds are likely to turn up and build their nests in this mustard tree. This thought can stretch our sometimes rather limited approach to the kingdom of God, represented here by the mustard tree.

Questions

What would you say makes up the DNA of the kingdom of God? How have you seen this DNA growing in your life? In the life of the community where you live, work and worship?

Stir each other to expand your thinking- just as the tree is large and has a variety of birds landing in it.

Response

What is your unique contribution to God's kingdom? How are you making that contribution? What is preventing you from making this contribution freely?

How can you make your contribution this week?

Pray for each other and the situations that you have just shared.

Fruitfulness

Bearing much fruit, John 15 : 8

'This is to my Father's glory, that you bear much fruit, showing yourselves to be my disciples.'

Read the whole of John 15:1-17, asking the group to notice the verses about bearing fruit.

As a visual example you could have a bowl of fruit or create a display of fruit on a coffee table on the centre of the room. If you want to expand this idea then branches with fruit on would be ideal and perhaps a pair of gardening secateurs and gloves.

Thoughts from this passage

Jesus is teaching his closest followers, preparing them for his death and their life afterwards. He uses a picture of the branches, together making up the vine, which would have been a familiar sight to those he was speaking to. There are many layers to this teaching but he uses the phrases 'remain in me' and 'remain in my love' seven times and links it each time with fruitfulness. It seems that fruitfulness has much to do with love and Jesus' command that we should love each other. The Father seems very involved with this vineyard, pruning and loving, loving and pruning. And Jesus' advice to his followers is to 'remaining in him', a key for us and a marker of God's kingdom.

In our world of targets and success, fruitfulness might be seen in terms of achievement, return on investment, focusing on numerical success - money, numbers involved in our programmes, size of our endeavours. For Jesus, fruitfulness was about loving one another. He probably knew that we would find this so difficult. We rub each other up the wrong way in our brokenness and differences.

We judge others and separate from them as we gather together with those who agree with us.

In verse 16, Jesus says that he chose his followers and appointed them to go and bear fruit - fruit that would last. You could say that the best of their fruit laid the foundation for two thousand years of telling the story of Jesus' life so that others could live this life of love.

Questions

How do you see fruitfulness?

What does it mean to you to 'remain in Jesus' and to 'remain in his love'?

Response

Facilitate a discussion where you explore as a group how this teaching is relevant to your lives today, as individuals and as a group? Make sure this is earthed in all your experience and leads to some commitment to change.

Remember to ask how members are getting on with this commitment in weeks to come.

Empowered to love

Matthew 5 : 43-47

'You have heard that it was said, "Love your neighbour and hate your enemy. But I tell you, love your enemies and pray for those who persecute you, that you may be children of your Father in heaven. He causes his sun to rise on the evil and the good, and sends rain on the righteous and the unrighteous. If you love those who love you, what reward will you get? Are not even the tax collectors doing that? And if you greet only your own people, what are you doing more than others? Do not even pagans do that?'

Read these verses to the group and ask the group for their first impressions of what this means.

Thoughts from this passage

This is one of the most challenging verses in the New Testament where Jesus asks us to love our enemies. In the kingdom of God no one is unlovable. Later on in the passage he tells us that anyone can love their friends and those they like, but he asks us to go beyond that.

Love in God's kingdom is the kind of love that changes marriages, changes all relationships in fact and changes the world. It is what makes the body of Christ really work and it gives us the motivation to reach out to those we come across with kindness and acceptance.

In other words what this passage is telling us to do is to love beyond our feelings.

It is when we have no positive feelings for people or situations that Christ's love begins. Our own love is just too limited. We can step into doing what is right despite our feelings, even when we would quite like to do nothing or do what is wrong.

So how do we do this? Recognising that these negative emotions are part of life is an honest place to start. When relationships go through hard times and situations are difficult, our emotional response is often defensive and blaming of others. We feel like these situations or people have become our enemies. They feel as if they are against us. Jesus set the high standard of love as he forgave those who were killing him. He asks us to do the same. To love those who feel against us. To refuse to dislike, hate even or to wish bad things for them. To love them anyway.

Questions

How would you describe people who have become your 'enemies'? What makes someone an enemy?

Jesus wouldn't have asked us to love our enemies if it were impossible. How can we love our enemies?

Response

In a time of silence, think of recent times when you have been forgiven. You can share these stories with the group if it feels appropriate.

Return to silence and ask the Lord to show you who has become your enemy. Make a list of all the things you need to forgive them for and offer this list to the Lord so he can help you to forgive them. This is often a process over weeks and months. The first step of loving our enemies can be an act of forgiveness.

Empowered discipleship

Romans 12 : 2

'*Do not conform to the pattern of this world, but be transformed by the renewing of your mind. Then you will be able to test and approve what God's will is—his good, pleasing and perfect will.*'

Read this verse through together a few times, noticing the verbs, the doing and being words in it.

You may want to print or write the verse out on a larger sheet of paper and look at it as a group and underline the doing and being words together.

Thoughts from this passage

When we think of discipleship we often think of choices, what I should or should not do or how I should or should not behave. By focusing on the verbs in the sentence we see that there is a pathway that leads us to know what is good, acceptable and perfect from God's point of view. From this base we will then know something of the will of God in our world. We will begin to value the things that he values and these values will motivate our choices and actions.

There are hugely significant questions that shape this journey.

In what ways am I conforming to the 'world'?

How is it possible for my thinking to be renewed?

What does this journey of transformation mean to me on a daily basis?

Am I discovering what God values and how can I learn to love these same things?

These are some of the questions that mark our way as disciples of Jesus. They change our understanding of being a Christian from following a list of rules to a life motivated by love.

Questions

Take each one of the questions above and ask the group to consider them prayerfully before discussing them together. This might take more than one group meeting. So you might want to just tackle one or two in this session and allow the group to go away and reflect and return to them the following week.

Response

What is my next step on this pathway of discipleship? Maybe it would be helpful to break into twos or threes for this conversation. Ask the group to be specific, practical and realistic in what they decide their next step should be. (Avoid the 'I should pray more' answer.)

You could return to the commitment made to these next steps at some point in the future to see how people are progressing.

For the full range of our
small group resources
visit our website: www.celluk.org.uk

Cracked pots...letting the light shine out

2 Corinthians 4 : 5-9

'For what we preach is not ourselves, but Jesus Christ as Lord, and ourselves as your servants for Jesus' sake. For God, who said, "Let light shine out of darkness," made his light shine in our hearts to give us the light of the knowledge of God's glory displayed in the face of Christ. But we have this treasure in jars of clay to show that this all-surpassing power is from God and not from us. We are hard pressed on every side, but not crushed; perplexed, but not in despair; persecuted, but not abandoned; struck down, but not destroyed.'

Read the passage slowly a couple of times, thinking about the concept of 'light'.

Thoughts from this passage

As an amateur potter who loves nothing more (except Jesus of course) than throwing pots on my potter's wheel, this passage is close to my heart. This is simply because it talks about 'earthen vessels' or as some versions say 'jars of clay'. As such I was fascinated to hear Paula Gooder (the resident theologian of the Bible Society) describe the two different types of pots available in Corinth at the time that Paul wrote this letter, making this a very powerful image in the minds of his fist century listeners. The first type was rather elegant, made of very fine clay, black in colour and expensive. The second type was made of poor quality, thrown to be very thin and because of this often had small cracks in them. As an amateur potter I am well acquainted with this kind of pot!

Paul is referring to this second type of pot. They were designed to have a candle placed inside them and the thin clay diffused the light and lit up the whole room! So Paul compares himself and indeed us to this type of fragile container. The links are clear. It is through our weakness that the inner light can most brightly shine.

So people were not meant to look at Paul and be impressed, but rather look through his weakness and see the inner light of God shining out. In our performance driven world I think this is quite a challenge to us as so often we want to be seen to be doing well and perhaps would prefer others to see us as the first type of pot available in Corinth.

Questions

How can we become more aware of God's presence in us?

Where do our weaknesses allow the light of God to shine through us?

Response

Which of these two pots do we most readily identify with? Reflect in silence for a couple of minutes about how much time and effort we put in to be an elegant pot? Why do we do this? Ask for feedback from the group after this silence if it seems appropriate.

Encourage each member of the group to spend a few moments in quiet asking God to reveal where an area of weakness has stopped them from allowing him to use them. We are often not very good at sharing our weaknesses. Encourage the group to be honest with themselves as they engage in the prayer in pairs. Share these and pray for each other.

Self-image

'For by the grace given me I say to every one of you: Do not think of yourself more highly than you ought, but rather think of yourself with sober judgment, in accordance with the faith God has distributed to each of you.'

'Therefore, if anyone is in Christ, the new creation has come;' 2 Corinthians 5:17

Thoughts from this passage

In the 1950s Dr Maxwell Maltz, a well-known plastic surgeon, noticed that when he did plastic surgery it often had a very positive impact on his patients' self-image, their confidence and what they felt they could or could not do. The effect of the surgery seemed out of all proportion to the actual intervention. Later he discovered that by helping people to think positively about themselves he didn't always have to do surgery as people accepted what they looked like. This too had a profoundly positive impact on their confidence and what they could or could not do.

We know that today many of us suffer from a low self-image, feelings of low self-worth. These feelings can rob us of the motivation to do certain things, leading sometimes to all sorts of negative and destructive behaviours. Psychologists say that these feelings are so powerful that they form a script, a repetitive message, which can control us in a negative way.

Rather than imagining yourself to be one of the beautiful, successful people so applauded in our world, how about imagining yourself receiving the loving gaze of God? What does he say about me? I am not the outcome of my successes and failures, my life's experience, but he sees me as his creation which he said was good. He couldn't love and accept me more than he does right now.

Questions

What is it that transforms the way we feel about ourselves? Is it being told that we are new creations or that we should think of ourselves with sober judgement - both of which are true - or something else?

What has been your experience of learning to love and accept yourself?

What would become possible if you could live from a deep knowledge of being loved and accepted?

Response

In learning to receive love, it is as if a light has been shone into our lives, revealing both goodness and the things in the shadows. How can we support each other as we journey with our shadow side; our fears, our shame and our anger?

A Prayer

'Father, I recognise that I am more than who my background says I am. I am not shaped by those negative things that have been said to me. I am a new creation, created and loved by you. Help me not to avoid my shadow side, but to have the courage to face those things which stop me from receiving your love and living as you would want me to.'

Encourage one another

Hebrews 10 : 23-25

'Let us hold unswervingly to the hope we profess, for he who promised is faithful. And let us consider how we may spur one another on toward love and good deeds, not giving up meeting together, as some are in the habit of doing, but encouraging one another—and all the more as you see the Day approaching.'

Thoughts from this passage

No one likes a moaning 'Minnie' (as my Mum calls them) or the Eeyores of this world as AA Milne characterises them. We can easily find ourselves drawn into rather negative conversations that pull us and others down. Picking holes in people or situations seems to be a regular past time for many. These verses ask us to do something completely different. As Christians we are called to be people of hope, people who believe in a God of the possible where change and redemption are real possibilities. One of the things I love about small groups is that they can be places of real encouragement where we can spur one another on as we seek to follow Jesus in our everyday lives.

Like most of the 'one another's' in the New Testament, this is set firmly in the context of a small group where open relationships and support can be fostered. The hope in these verses are not based on anything we might have done or plan to do, but on what God has done, 'for he who promised is faithful'.

A friend once described my own gift of encouragement as a bit like 'a poke with a sharp stick!' A prod to action you might say. A deliberate attempt to get someone to do something that they may be a little reluctant to do, but which will ultimately be good for them and those around them. In this way we are stimulating courage in those that we seek to encourage.

Questions

What are these 'love and good deeds' that these verses focus on? Are you drawn to particular sorts of loving and good deeds?

When did you last experience a 'poke with a sharp stick'? What was the outcome?

We all receive encouragement in different ways. How would it be helpful for members of your group to encourage you?

Response

Share current situations where you feel you are in need of encouragement. Include the ways in which you can increase the love and good works that the passage highlights so the situations have a practical outcome.

What would you like the Lord to help you with? Ask for his encouragement and notice the encouragement that comes in all sorts of creative ways between now and when you next meet as a group. Remember to ask for feedback next time you meet.

Also think of areas where you could encourage others this coming week, make sure these are genuine and thoughtful. Notice the difference it makes.

Blessed to be a blessing

Genesis 12 : 1-3

The Lord had said to Abram, "Go from your country, your people and your father's household to the land I will show you. 'I will make you into a great nation, and I will bless you; I will make your name great, and you will be a blessing. I will bless those who bless you, and whoever curses you I will curse; and all peoples on earth will be blessed through you.'

Read the passage and ask the group what strikes them about it?

Thoughts from this passage

In this passage we see something of the heart of God and his desire to bless all people. Although God could do this perfectly well on his own, he chooses to involve Abram in his plan. Why would God do this? Doesn't it just complicate things and mean that they may not happen in the way that he imagines? Surely an almighty and all powerful God would not need to take this sort of risk? What we see here is that God chooses to use Abram. In the same way he chooses to use us in his plans. Just as he chose Abraham, so in Jesus he has chosen us.

God, whose essence is love, chooses to work in partnership with us. This is an expression of his love. By blessing us he says that we also should be a blessing to others, in this way we are expressing God's love to those who we choose to bless. Abram hears God's words and obeys them and the rest as we say is history!

Questions

What does this word 'blessing' mean to you and how have you experienced God's blessings? (Sometimes 'blessings' are hard won - Abram had to leave his home and face childlessness for example. Not necessarily things we would count as experiences leading to blessing.)

Response

Make a list of the blessings we as individuals have received in all sorts of ways, in our work, relationships, beliefs. The list is long. Share these together with the group and celebrate them.

In verse 3 there is an implication that we are all a conduit of blessing. As we are blessed, we will bless others. Discuss as a group how you can bless others in the ways that you have received blessings from God. Be practical and specific. Find something you can do, as well as noticing who you can be. Also note any themes through the whole group. Is there something we can bless others with as a group?

Anticipate moments in the next week when you might have the opportunity to bless others. Share these anticipated moments and pray for each other that you will be a blessing to those who you come in contact with. Also be aware that there will be unexpected times over and above these were you can be spontaneous.

rather be blessed or be a blessing?
to what (place, pple, priority) might God be calling you?

Having co-workers

Colossians 4 : 10-12

'My fellow prisoner Aristarchus sends you his greetings, as does Mark, the cousin of Barnabas. (You have received instructions about him; if he comes to you, welcome him.) Jesus, who is called Justus, also sends greetings. These are the only Jews among my co-workers for the kingdom of God, and they have proved a comfort to me. Epaphras, who is one of you and a servant of Christ Jesus, sends greetings. He is always wrestling in prayer for you, that you may stand firm in all the will of God, mature and fully assured.'

Ask one of the group to read the passage, have a time of quiet to let it settle and then ask them to read it again.

Thoughts from this passage

Oh no, it's one of those lists of names and at least some of them are going to be impossible to pronounce! Let's just skip this bit. It was obviously only directly relevant to the people of that time in Paul's circle of friends. But wait a moment. Perhaps there are some things we can learn here. It shows us very clearly that Paul was in a team. He had 'co-workers for the kingdom of God'. What we also see is that these workers where a diverse band, some Jews and some Gentiles. We also see that they are in different locations and travel between regions. They are also in touch with each other's needs, hence Epaphras 'wrestling in prayer for them'.

We catch a glimpse here of how relational and interconnected the early church was. They didn't think of themselves as 'lone rangers'. For many of us today it can feel a bit as if we are on our own as a Christian in the work place, our family or our local community. Just like Paul, we need to have co-workers who will cheer us on, comfort us and wrestle in prayer for us so that we can stand firm.

Questions

What is Paul talking about when he calls people his 'co-workers for the kingdom of God'? He could have called them friends, but there seems to be another dimension here.

Who would you identify as having been your co-workers for the kingdom in the past? What role did they play for you?

Response

Are there ways that members of the group can work as co-workers? Talk about the support you can give each other, picking up on some of the issues raised by the passage.

What are the areas that you need to 'wrestle in prayer' over for each other? Be honest and share the things that you are finding particularly challenging as you consider the kingdom of God in your life. How can you pray for each other in a meaningful way?

Take some time to pray together over what has come up. If it feels appropriate stand and join hands together as a sign of your partnership in the Kingdom and pray a blessing over the group.

Prayer

1 Timothy 2 : 1

'I urge, then, first of all, that petitions, prayers, intercession and thanksgiving be made for all people-'

Thoughts from this passage

There are a number of different forms of prayer that are outlined in this passage. The word 'prayer' as it is used here is the word to 'pour out'. This speaks of the devotional side of our prayer lives, by which I mean where we are not asking on behalf of other people. We are not necessarily asking for things at all. It is about our soul, our life and what we are going through.

In the Psalms we get an amazing glimpse into David's prayer life. Many of these Psalms are in the nature of prayers. They record David pouring out what he is involved in and how he feels. They are quite surprising; they are negative, raw, questioning the presence of God and his love. They deal with the 'nitty gritty' and emotion of his everyday life. Psalm 10 is a good example of this and starts with the shout 'Oh God, where are you?' which I am sure we have all echoed at some time in our life.

This speaks to me about telling God everything, what we are honestly going through, our difficulties, our inappropriate thoughts, anger etc. The things we are ashamed about.

We know we can be honest about these things with God as we share our shame, our raw emotions and our questions as to whether God is with us or not. The pattern in Psalm 10 is that the psalmist pours out his negativity and pain but in the end he declares that God is with him.

Honestly opening our hearts to God builds relationship with him. Knowing his love for us, we can receive forgiveness which is the beginning of our transformation and strengthening.

Questions

What does the word 'prayer' mean to you?

How have you found it most helpful to build a relationship with God?

What do you think is the next step for you in developing your relationship with God?

Outcomes and Application

Lead a time of thanksgiving for the steps along the way with God and the keys you have all learnt that help with this journey. If you have time you could give the group paper and felt tips and ask them to draw their journey marking the highlights, the learning times, the times of struggle.

What emerges from reflection of this picture?

Prayer Cards
This is a dynamic way to use the Lord's prayer and bring creative energy to your small group as you pray together. These cards can also be used by individuals in their own lives to give an effective pattern to their prayer life. Order online at www.celluk.org.uk

Prayer for others

'I urge, then, first of all, that petitions, prayers, intercession and thanksgiving be made for all people-'

Thoughts from this passage

In this verse we are introduced to the idea of intercession where we pray for others. We step into situations, some of which we might be personally involved in - praying for family and friends, for our neighbours and our town. Some might be praying for situations far away; for issues in the world of injustice, poverty and conflict. The possibilities for our intercession are simply endless as we see the needs in the world and our helplessness. We need you God.

What are the challenges we face as we intercede for others? For example, finding the energy and motivation to pray. There may be many reasons for why this is difficult. It can be a real death to self. Sometimes it is hard to do the work of discovering how we can best pray, rather than just presuming our best thoughts into the situation are right and enough. We have to grapple with past experiences of apparently unanswered prayer.

Another reason might be because much of our prayer is a mystery.

Why would our almighty and loving God apparently need our prayers for him to act in this world of his? How can we know what he is up to? Indeed how interventionist is our God?

Could it be that needing answers to these deep questions leads us away from that childlike faith of 'we don't understand but we do need you God?'

However, Jesus does ask us to pray that God's will be done so that his kingdom can come on earth. The challenge it seems to me is to be able to differentiate between my best thoughts and the will of God. If we are to pray in Jesus name we need to be somewhat confident that our prayers, especially if we are asking for specifics, might be an echo of what he would want. Some things we can know. For example everything about God is loving, so our intercessions need to line up with love of all parties involved as well as the created world.

Questions

What values of God other than love need to determine our intercessions?

How can we come in humility to our intercessions? For example, having a time of silence before we speak so that we can lay aside our agenda and listen to God.

Response

Share your experience with each other and the wisdom you have learnt when coming to intercession. Perhaps the group could make a new commitment to end each small group meeting with ten minutes of defined intercession for your friends, your neighbours, your town, the world .

Hearing God in ordinary places

Jeremiah 18 : 1-6

'This is the word that came to Jeremiah from the LORD: "Go down to the potter's house, and there I will give you my message." So I went down to the potter's house, and I saw him working at the wheel. But the pot he was shaping from the clay was marred in his hands; so the potter formed it into another pot, shaping it as seemed best to him. Then the word of the LORD came to me. He said, "Can I not do with you, Israel, as this potter does?" declares the LORD. "Like clay in the hand of the potter, so are you in my hand, Israel.'

Have a selection of pottery items set out as you read the passage. These could be bowls, vases, cups etc. A variety of shapes and sizes of items would be helpful.

Thoughts from this passage

Jeremiah heard from God, 'go down to the potter's house'. On reflection a slightly strange request from God to go to a place of work and hear from him! Not the sort of place we would normally go to hear from God. Jeremiah obeys and heads down to the potter's house. Interesting that Jeremiah is used to hearing God's voice, recognises and acts on it. The next thing to note is that God speaks to him as he watches the potter at work at his wheel throwing a pot. Through this everyday activity God speaks very clearly to Jeremiah. The potter however is not having such a good day! The clay he is working with is marred in his hands, this could be due to a lump in the clay, an air bubble or grit of some sort. I wonder if the air went blue as the potter got frustrated with the clay!

Somehow Jeremiah knew that all was not well with the potter and the clay, and watches as another pot is shaped from this marred clay as the potter sees fit. Notice the sequence. Jeremiah reflects on what he sees and then says, 'then the word of the Lord came to me'. So God spoke after he had watched, as Jeremiah was reflecting on what he had seen.

Questions

What strikes you most about this story?

What would it take for you to be more open to hear God in ordinary places?

Response

How have you experienced God shaping your life? You could share times when God has spoken to you through particular circumstances.

Lead a time of reflection

Ask the group to move into silence and having done so suggest that they look at the pottery items you have on display. Spend 5-10 minutes looking deeply at the shapes, asking God to speak to you about how he sees you or how he sees a situation you are concerned about. Share afterwards what people have experienced.

Guidance

This way...

Acts 8 : 4-40

Read Acts 8:4-40 to the group and ask yourselves these four questions:

What guidance did Philip have to leave Jerusalem?
What guidance did he have to start preaching the gospel in Samaria?
What guidance did he have to leave the revival and go into the desert?
What guidance did he have to speak to the Ethiopian in the chariot?

Thoughts from this passage

In this passage we get a look into the life of Philip and his journey. What has always interested me is what we can learn about his decision making processes. Over the years two questions have been asked of me again and again, does God love me and how can I know that I am doing the right thing. How does God guide me? It is the second of these questions that we can learn something from Philip in this story. He leaves Jerusalem for Samaria, fleeing for his life when persecution broke out. He didn't need guidance, circumstances motivated his action. It was go or die. He would have needed specific guidance to stay. When he gets there he begins to preach the gospel and many responded. What guidance did he have? Jesus told everybody to be a witness and Philip was simply living by this principle, being obedient.

We learn that most of the time our guidance is to live by the principles that Jesus taught and demonstrated. The principles and values of the kingdom of God as communicated through our understanding of scripture. We have also been given the ability to think. We take what we know and reason it out. We take responsibility for our decisions and do the work necessary to make good choices, made from the principles gained from life and scripture.

However, in the midst of this revival Philip is told by an Angel to go into the desert. This is a different kind of guidance. There may be a few times in our lives where God wants us to do something specific so he speaks loud enough for us to hear. Here he speaks the loudest he can by sending an angel, because if you were in the middle of a revival you would not leave unless you had real certainty - angels do that! Then he finds himself in the desert and comes across a chariot. This time he doesn't need an angel. He is prompted by the spirit. Maybe in his travels he has learnt more about hearing that small voice. He acts on the principle of 'loving your neighbour' and finds the Ethiopian open to God in a startling way.

It is comforting to know that if we need a change of direction God will speak loud enough for us to hear. Otherwise he has given us the principles to make these decisions and he wants us to take responsibility for our choice. Sometimes the invitation from him is simply 'what would you like to do', 'what would bring life to you?' Sometimes he doesn't seem to mind saying 'I will be with you anyway'.

Questions

What has been your experience of making decisions?

Are there stories from the group about supernatural guidance where they have had a prompt from the Holy Spirit, or a prophecy?

Response

Ask the group to tell their stories about how they made a decision by scriptural principle and life experience.

If there are current situations for group members who are struggling to make a decision spend some time sharing these things and praying for them.

Our view of people

2 Corinthians 5 : 14-15

'For Christ's love compels us, because we are convinced that one died for all and therefore all died. And he died for all, that those who live should no longer live for themselves but for him who died for them and was raised again.'

Thoughts from the passage

Life defining moments for all of us are rare but important. In the 1970s as a very young Christian I was a member of a Christian community looking to do good things in the community. Our leader Lorraine ran a drop-in shelter for young people who were members of a local gang, their age range was from about 8 to 16 and one or two other children tagged along.

One day she asked me to lead this group as she was unable to be there, warning me that I was to be aware of one of the boys who was very dirty. I was to love him regardless, which might prove quite difficult. Thinking that a little mud could hardly be a problem, I sailed into the situation. When this young boy came up to me for a hug the difficulty clearly presented itself. He was soaked in urine and had soiled his underwear. Lorraine had told me earlier that whatever happened I was not to clean up this boy. If he was clean his parents beat him up. I was to accept him as he was. Sadly, all I could do was turn my back on him and walk away.

In discussing this later with Lorraine she pointed out this passage in 2 Corinthians 5:15. Firstly mentioning verse 14, 'for the love of Christ calls us, because we are convinced that one has died for all'.

She said that every person has value because we are all created in God's image and are loved by him. This is demonstrated in this verse by the fact that 'Christ died for all' My challenge was to no longer look from a human perspective, from the outside, but to ask God for a big heart to see this young person as they really are in his sight. If I did that I would able to love this lad. So I prayed and the next time I met him, by the grace of God, I looked beyond that dirt. I was able to engage with him and play with him no matter what state he was in.

Questions

What do you think are the principles behind this story?

Is anyone beyond being treated with respect?

Response

Ask the group to reflect together on times when they have felt disrespected. Maybe they have felt patronised or dismissed, not listened to or misunderstood. How did that feel?

Bring these situations and the feelings they aroused to God for healing, remembering to spend time receiving his love which is never disrespectful.

For the full range of our
small group resources
visit our website: www.celluk.org.uk

Our view of people in the workplace

Matthew 5 : 13

'You are the salt of the earth. But if the salt loses its saltiness, how can it be made salty again? It is no longer good for anything, except to be thrown out and trampled underfoot.'

Thoughts from this passage

What was Jesus saying about us in this statement which comes at the end of the Beatitudes? Salt preserves and adds taste - it makes a difference. You don't need much salt for it to do its job. It was very valuable in the ancient world. Roman soldiers were paid in salt at times - when they were 'worth their salt'. Christians who live out the Beatitudes are valuable and will make a difference to those around them. To be effective we must be in contact with those who we live and work amongst, involved in showing mercy, bringing peace and upholding justice. This requires treating those we come across with respect as people loved by God and valuable to him.

The great writer C.S. Lewis was once asked what heaven would be like. Strangely he answered that he thought it would be very polite and people would have good manners. To start with this may sound somewhat ridiculous, but the more you think about it the deeper it gets. Surely what he meant was that we will see the real value of people in all their wonder and we will treat each other with great love and respect.

In our workplace having this high value of people makes a difference. A friend of mine was challenged by this thought. Every day at his work place he walked past ten people's desks between the lift and his office. Basically having ignored these people for many years, he was not entirely sure who they were or what they did. On this day of challenge he stopped by a desk and introduced himself. Every day he introduced himself to a new person. On his birthday he bought cakes. When one of them was sick, he sent flowers. Slowly he changed the experience of working there because he had changed his perception of these people. Small things can mean a lot.

Questions

What are the attributes of people who Jesus described as 'salt of the earth'? You might find it helpful to read the passage from Matthew chapter 5 which comes before this verse.

Not only Christians are in essence 'salty'. How can we be inspired to have a high view of people, all people?

Response

Discuss in the group what environments you could change by having this high view of people.

Ask each member to share an area they are involved in where they could change the atmosphere by the way they value people.

The unknown God

'While Paul was waiting for them in Athens, he was greatly distressed to see that the city was full of idols. So he reasoned in the synagogue with both Jews and God-fearing Greeks, as well as in the marketplace day by day with those who happened to be there. A group of Epicurean and Stoic philosophers began to debate with him. Some of them asked, "What is this babbler trying to say?" Others remarked, "He seems to be advocating foreign gods." They said this because Paul was preaching the good news about Jesus and the resurrection. Then they took him and brought him to a meeting of the Areopagus, where they said to him, "May we know what this new teaching is that you are presenting? You are bringing some strange ideas to our ears, and we would like to know what they mean." (All the Athenians and the foreigners who lived there spent their time doing nothing but talking about and listening to the latest ideas.)'

'Paul then stood up in the meeting of the Areopagus and said: "People of Athens! I see that in every way you are very religious. For as I walked around and looked carefully at your objects of worship, I even found an altar with this inscription: to an unknown god. So you are ignorant of the very thing you worship—and this is what I am going to proclaim to you."'

Thoughts from this passage

Paul is in Athens and addresses the people who live in Athens very specifically about what he observes.

This leads to an invitation for Paul to explain his ideas about Jesus. Those Greeks loved to debate - maybe they worshipped new ideas! Every culture has gods that it worships. Even though our current culture is often described as secular, we still have gods and idols that are worshipped. Paul takes time to 'walk around and look carefully' at their objects of worship.

Questions

How do you recognise what is worshipped in our culture?

What are the specific gods in our culture?

Make a list of those things that our culture treats as gods or idols.

In what ways are these 'gods' worshipped?

Response

Are you guilty of worshipping some of the gods in our culture? Have a moment of silence for personal thought? If appropriate ask for feedback.

Spend some time discussing as a group how we can sensitively highlight the gods and idols we have listed above. How can we share the gospel in an appropriate way in light of these findings? Think about how the gospel connects particularly with what we have found.

Encourage one another to look for opportunities for conversations in the next week around the idols of our culture.

People of peace

Luke 10 : 1-6

'*After this the Lord appointed seventy-two others and sent them two by two ahead of him to every town and place where he was about to go. He told them, "The harvest is plentiful, but the workers are few. Ask the Lord of the harvest, therefore, to send out workers into his harvest field. Go! I am sending you out like lambs among wolves. Do not take a purse or bag or sandals; and do not greet anyone on the road. "When you enter a house, first say, 'Peace to this house.' 6 If someone who promotes peace is there, your peace will rest on them; if not, it will return to you.*'

Read the passage and ask the group to imagine themselves being one of the seventy in the story as it is read. Pause for a few moments and ask them to share their reflections.

Thoughts from this passage

There are a number of areas we could look at in this passage but I just want to focus on two.

Firstly, Jesus says 'the harvest is plentiful.' There isn't a problem with the harvest. There is plenty of it. Jesus does not ask us to pray for the harvest but he does ask us to pray for labourers. Who are these labourers? It is the seventy that he has appointed who are the ones that Jesus tells to go (verse 3).

Just as Jesus sends out these labourers so he also sends us out. Maybe we are in the habit of waiting for people to come to us. Here it is quite clear that we are to go.

Secondly, Jesus tells the disciples to find 'people of peace'. We can understand this as meaning people who are open to them and their message about Jesus. Not only are they to find them but stay with them. In this way they are building relationships and in doing so preparing the way for the message of Jesus.

Questions

How did you become open to the gospel message and as such became a person of peace?

How will you recognise a person of peace?

Response

What has been your experience of this plentiful harvest? Some members of the group might have had difficult experiences when they tried to share their message of the love of God, finding the harvest far from plentiful. It would be good to get these out in the open and try to build hope again.

Discuss who in your network of friendships might be a person of peace? How will you approach these people—maybe even in the week ahead?

Make the most of every opportunity

Colossians 4 : 2-6

'Devote yourselves to prayer, being watchful and thankful. And pray for us, too, that God may open a door for our message, so that we may proclaim the mystery of Christ, for which I am in chains. Pray that I may proclaim it clearly, as I should. Be wise in the way you act toward outsiders; make the most of every opportunity. Let your conversation be always full of grace, seasoned with salt, so that you may know how to answer everyone.'

Thoughts from this passage

Have you ever explained something to someone and detected that they have not understood it - maybe a practical task at work, an instruction to a child or in conversation with your spouse? I am sure it is a common occurrence for many of us. As it is often said, communication is a two way thing. There is a deliverer and a receiver. Paul knew this and asked for prayer in both the delivery and reception of his vital message. His phrase 'open a door for our message' has the receiver as its focus, 'pray that I may proclaim it clearly' has the deliverer in mind.

It is good to recognise that we are not alone in our struggle to speak to people about the love of God. We are indeed in good company if the apostle Paul found this a challenge and asked others to pray for him. Let's be real about this. At this time in our culture we meet few who are ready and open to hear our traditional message. We have to earn the right to speak about the God we know by demonstrating authentic, unconditional love, usually over a long period, before we can break down the stereotypes of Christians. We have to understand the messages in our culture so we can speak in a way that is relevant and helpful. Perhaps our message needs to come from a different angle than when we heard it and responded. Paul found ways of speaking about God in each of the places he visited. He used his own story but with a cultural bias to capture the attention of those he spoke to. Also he made sure he was wise in the way he acted toward outsiders in order to make the most of every opportunity. He suggests that we let our conversation be always full of grace, seasoned with salt, so that you may know how to answer everyone.

Questions

How should we speak about God in our culture? What is relevant to our friends and contacts? Does the message of sin and redemption still communicate?
Where are the open doors or slightly open doors for our message in our situation?
What might be the reason for people not being open?

Response

How can we be confident that our encounters will always be full of grace? What do these conversations that are 'seasoned with salt' mean to you?
How does fear hold you back from speaking? Explore together what stops you making the most of every opportunity or perhaps even creating opportunities.

If your group is ready then pray for each other both for opportunities to share the gospel but also skill to do that clearly and well. Take a few moments to allow each person in the group to bring someone to mind who they may have an opportunity to share with. Commit to being more open to hearing God this coming week and make plans to share situations where you have encountered him next time you meet together.

The power of questions ??

Mark 8 : 27-29

Jesus and his disciples went on to the villages around Caesarea Philippi. On the way he asked them, "Who do people say I am?" They replied, "Some say John the Baptist; others say Elijah; and still others, one of the prophets." "But what about you?" he asked. "Who do you say I am?" Peter answered, "You are the Messiah."'

Thoughts from this passage

In his book 'Jesus Asked What He Wanted To Know', Conrad Gempf highlighted that in the first Gospel which is attributed to Mark there are sixty seven episodes in which there is conversation. Jesus asks an astonishing fifty questions in those episodes. I think this gives us a fascinating insight into the way Jesus worked. Of all people he had some pretty important things to say. However he spends time asking questions.

As we can see in the verses above, Jesus is interested in who the disciples and others said he was. He could just have told them. Surely that would have been easier and a far more effective way of getting the point across. Perhaps we can conclude that getting the point across was not Jesus' main goal here. In asking questions he was getting others to think for themselves and to find an answer.

Questions

So what can we take from this and the other encounters that Jesus has where he asks questions? Here are a few thoughts. In asking questions we awake people's curiosity and get them thinking as the disciples had to in this passage. Questions give us a real insight into what people are thinking, rather than assuming they have the same understanding about something as we do. Good questions can unearth blind spots in people's world view and give opportunities for a different world view to be accepted or sought. Here is a question that I like to use in this respect: 'Is the world as it should be and if not why not?'

Response

'Who do you say that I am?'

In pairs use the question above and ask each other to answer it without using religious language or Christian jargon.

Think of questions you could ask friends that would stimulate a conversation about faith. Try them out in the same pairs as before.

Commit together to take opportunities to ask questions over this coming week and report back next time you are together.

For the full range of our small group resources visit our website: www.celluk.org.uk

Hospitality

Hebrews 13 : 2

'Do not forget to show hospitality to strangers, for by so doing some people have shown hospitality to angels without knowing it.'

Read this verse to the group, ask the group for their first impression and write it down.

Thoughts from this passage

Throughout the Bible God's people are challenged to be hospitable, mostly to strangers. This verse in Hebrews emphasises its importance The story of the Good Samaritan from Luke 10: 25-37 is about acts of mercy and practical hospitality. Hospitality became a fundamental part of early church life. Aristides, one of the early church fathers described a common practice. 'When they meet strangers, they invite them to their homes with joy, for they recognise them as true brothers, not natural, but spiritual.'

In our world today people are cynical about words, only believing what they see and experience. Recent research reported in 'Talking Jesus' (www.talkingjesus.org) shows that people come to faith through the influence of friends. Hospitality is often the first step of a relationship and a friendship. The invitation for a cup of coffee, a glass of wine, a meal whether in your own home or in the local coffee shop, is powerful.

What do these simple acts of hospitality and friendship show? Perhaps two important things.

Firstly, it shows the big heartedness of the person offering hospitality, which for us is an expression of what we believe God to be like. Everything in our creation shows a generous big hearted God. Secondly, hospitality conveys value to the person who is receiving it.

A few years ago I was asked to do some teaching on evangelism for a church. I spent the first hour talking about hospitality. In the break the church leaders expressed some unhappiness with my subject matter as he had asked me to speak on evangelism. I told him that hospitality was the new evangelism. It is at the heart of our response to our world. Including people in our lives through acts of hospitality is powerful.

Questions

According to Alan Krieder (Resident But Alien: How the Early Church Grew), hospitality was a major contribution in the evangelisation of the Roman world. What is the role of hospitality now?

What makes someone a hospitable person?

Response

What is your view of embracing hospitality in a greater way in your life? Think for a moment of one or two people who perhaps you could reach out to by inviting them for coffee or a meal; a neighbour, an acquaintance, someone at work.

The truth is that any act of sacrifice on our time and energy can be difficult so let's ask God for his help in this, whatever we are finding the barriers to hospitality.

Other resources

40 Creative Worship Ideas for Small Groups
In each of these tins we have brought together 40 worship ideas which anybody doing small groups will find helpful. These fantastic worship ideas are each printed on a card with a picture and are presented in a set of 40 in an attractive tin. They have been organised into six streams that reflect historical streams of our Christian faith: contemplative, holiness, charismatic, social justice, evangelical, incarnational.

40 More Creative Worship Ideas for Small Groups
Our second set of worship ideas also covers a broad range of Christian worship. We all connect with God in different ways, so these sets of cards each contain a range of ideas with the hope that everyone in your group can lead worship confidently. They have been organised into eight streams: Our lives, Scripture, Objects, Words, The natural world, Games, 'I am' sayings of Jesus and Stories behind the hymns.

40 Missional Ideas for Small Groups
How can each one of us live out Christ in the context of where we work, where we live and in our families? Cell UK has brought together 40 fantastic ideas for use in small groups. Each idea takes about 15 minutes and gives practical ways to encourage and empower each other as we seek to love those around us and share Jesus with them. The ideas in this set of postcards, presented in a high quality durable tin, break down into 8 themes each taking your small group on a journey, renewing minds and creating new rhythms for life.

Other resources

Small Groups—an Introduction
Laurence Singlehurst
This booklet seeks to give some biblical background and framework along with a practical understanding of what it might be like to be part of a small group. Suitable for those joining or starting a group, or for those already in one to refresh your understanding of what it means to be in a small group.

Empowering People
Laurence Singlehurst
Laurence Singlehurst is asked all the time what have we learnt in the last 20 years about holistic small groups with a missional heartbeat, sometimes called cells? In this booklet he answers the questions: what has worked? What has not worked? What is the legacy? And 'Am I positive about the future?' This booklet contains lessons learned and ideas for the future to give churches and individuals the best practice for small groups. This booklet is also available as a free PDF download at www.celluk.org.uk.

Help! I'm Leading Part of my Small Group
Trevor Withers
This booklet has been revised and updated. Designed to help small group members who are leading one of the sections of the meeting on any occasion. The aim is to increase the understanding of what should be happening in each of the sections and give practical ideas and help that will make the section you are leading a success.

Other resources

4Life
Mark Powley
Want to go deeper with God or refresh your faith? 4Life is full of honesty, passion and humour, and seeks to give a solid foundation for practical Christian living today. The ingredients are simple; ten readings on your own, then an honest meeting with a trusted mentor. The journey in these pages will leave you changed.

4Life Group Notes
Mark Powley
This booklet seeks to give some biblical background and framework along with a practical understanding of what it might be like to be part of a small group. Suitable for those joining or starting a group, or for those already in one to refresh your understanding of what it means to be in a small group.

To purchase our books and resources and for information about our training days and courses visit our website at www.celluk.org.uk

Or phone: 01582 463330
email: cellukresources@oval.com

About the authors

Laurence Singlehurst
Laurence led Youth with a Mission for over a decade. He currently leads Cell UK, is on the Hope leadership team and is Chairman of the Board of Trustees for Westminster Theology College. Laurence is passionate about the potential of/championing peer leadership amongst young people and training young emerging speakers. He is an author, speaker, and antique collector/history buff.

Trevor Withers
Trevor leads the leadership team of Network Church St Albans as well as working alongside Laurence Singlehurst at Cell UK. He also runs a small business and has a pottery studio and garden railway for fun. He is passionate about small groups.

Liz West
Our grateful thanks to Liz, our patient and long -suffering editor who has been a faithful friend and fellow worker in the kingdom to both of the authors for many years.

Notes

Pictures used in this publication are from the following sources:

Page 6   Mustard seed jmiltenburg /Mourgue file

Page 8   Plums/P. Kinahan

Page 10   Spray heart/Morgue file

Page 12   Walking together/Cell UK

Page 14   Cracked pots/T. Withers

Page 16   Reflection Javi-indy/Freepik.com

Page 18   Thumbs up Luis_molinero/Freepik.com

Page 20   Gift ribbon and bow/Kstudio-Freepik.com

Page 22   Team work Jcomp/Freepik.com

Page 24   Belief Katemangostar/Freepik.com

Page 26   Forest bridge Welcomier/Freepik.com

Page 28   Potters hands/M. Withers

Page 30   White sign Vivash/Freepik.com

Page 32   Christ on the cross Kjpargeter
              - Freepik.com

Page 34   Salt/Morguefile.com

Page 36   Greek pillars/Kconnors Morguefile.com

Page 38   Harvest field/P.Kinahan

Page 40   Door way/T.Withers

Page 44   Tea pot/G.Kelham